W9-DHT-656

NICE AND CLEAN
Anne and Harlow Rockwell

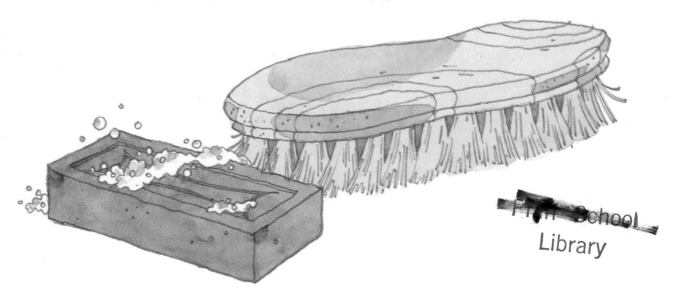

Macmillan Publishing Company · New York

Macmillan Publishing Company
866 Third Avenue, New York, N.Y. 10022
Collier Macmillan Canada, Inc.

Printed in the United States of America

10   9   8   7   6   5   4   3   2

Library of Congress Cataloging in Publication Data

Rockwell, Anne.
  Nice and clean.

  Summary: Presents the many devices and implements—
from mop and broom to scouring pad and silver polish—
that are used in cleaning the house.
  1. House cleaning—Equipment and supplies—Juvenile
literature. [1. House cleaning—Equipment and supplies]
I. Rockwell, Harlow. II. Title.
TX324.R62 1984   648'.5   84-3945
ISBN 0-02-777290-X

648
R

7/9/90 Follett 11) 0'

Do you know how we clean our house?

10051

We wash our dirty dishes in the sink.

We dry the glasses with a dishtowel
and we let the other dishes dry
in the drying rack.

We scrub the pots and pans
with a scouring pad until they are shiny bright.

The kitchen garbage goes in the plastic bag inside the garbage can.
The waste paper goes in the wastebasket.

We sweep the floor with a broom.

The sweepings go in the dustpan.

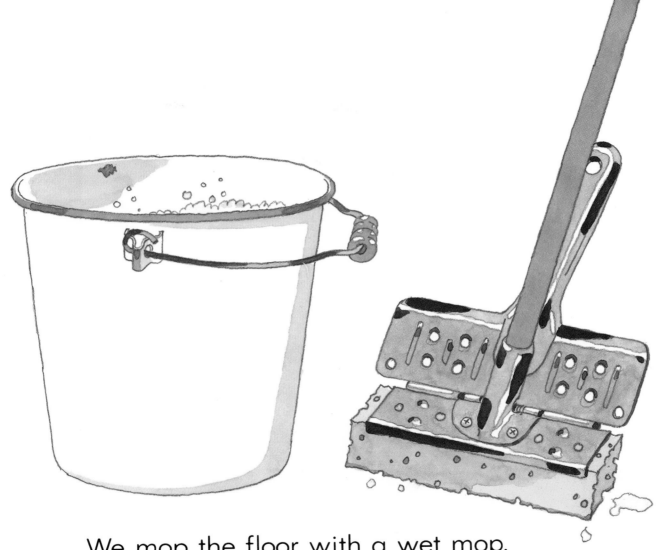

We mop the floor with a wet mop.

We wash our windows with ammonia and water.
I don't like the way ammonia smells.

We iron our curtains with an iron
on an ironing board.
The iron is hot.

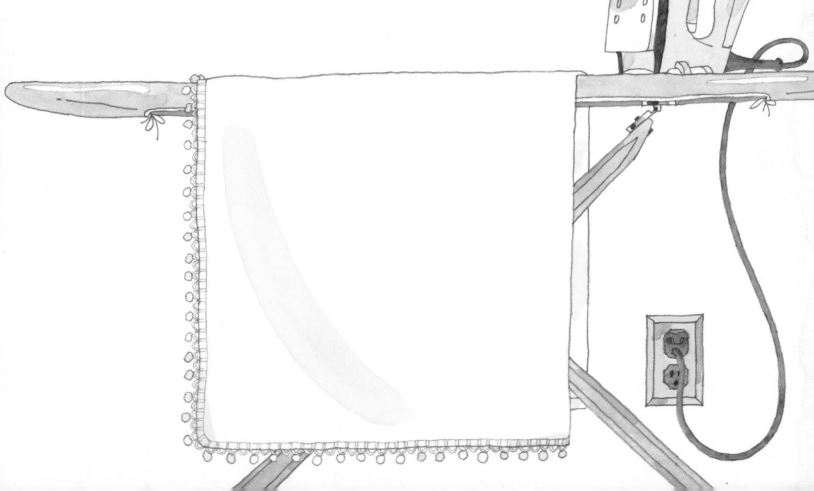

The dustcloth and feather duster
are for dusting.

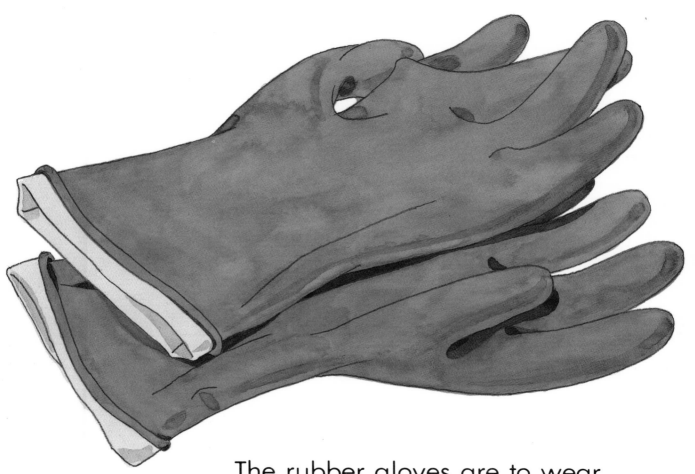

The rubber gloves are to wear
when we clean the oven.

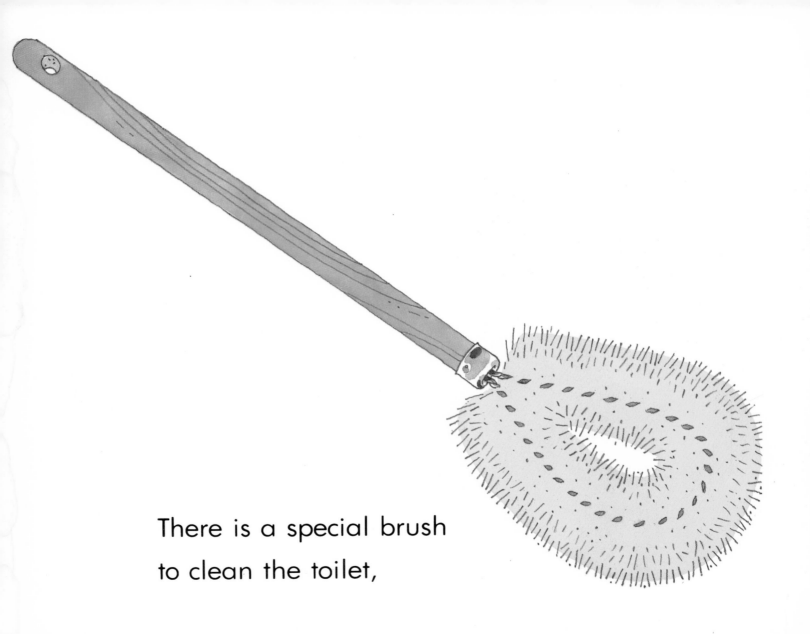

There is a special brush
to clean the toilet,

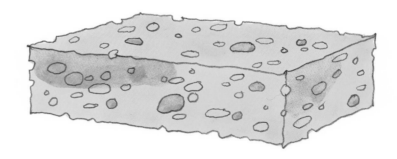

and scouring powder and a sponge
to clean the bathtub and sink.

The vacuum cleaner cleans our carpet.

It rolls on wheels and makes a loud, loud noise.

Our cat doesn't like it.

We polish our furniture
with furniture polish.

We wax our floors with wax.

We have so many things
for cleaning our house!

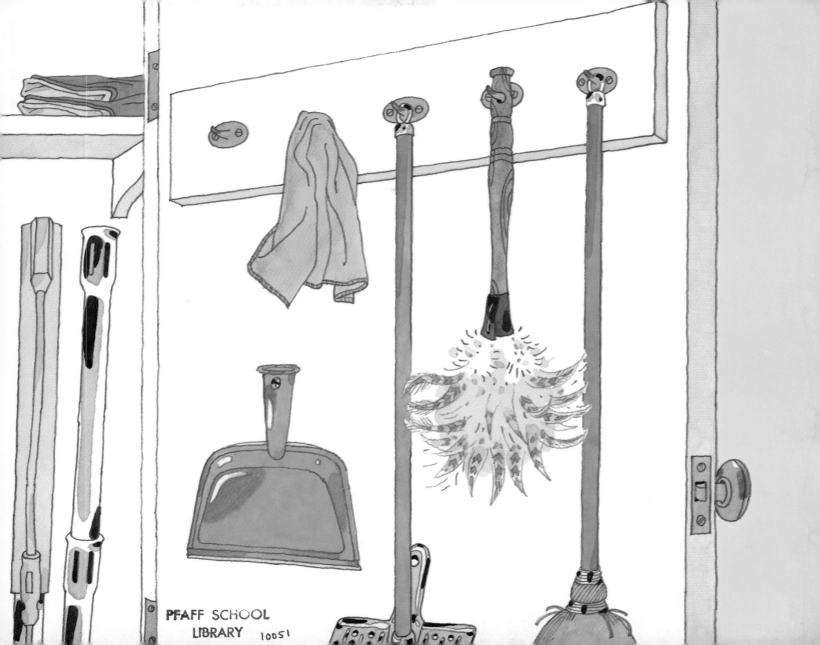

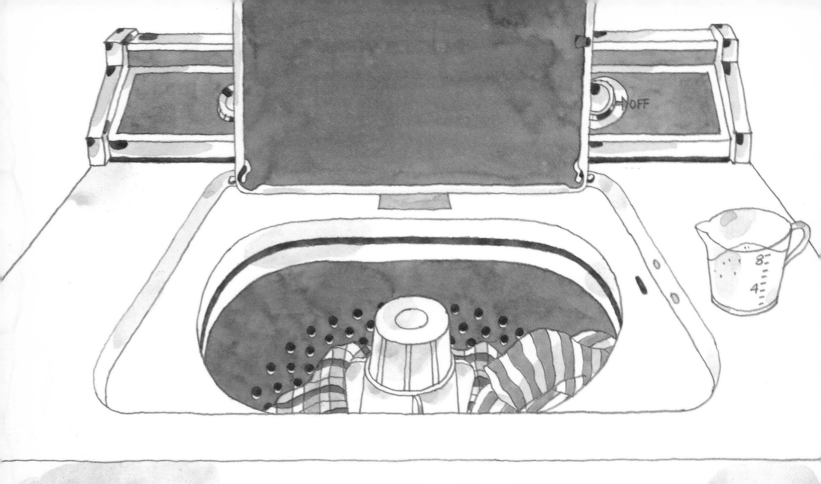

And we have a washer and dryer
to wash and dry our clothes

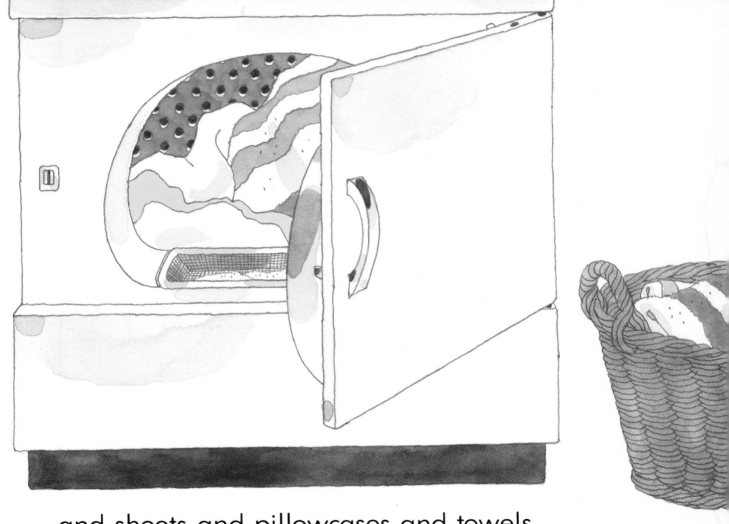

and sheets and pillowcases and towels
and washcloths and dustcloths and curtains, too.

Everything in our house is nice and clean.

And I am, too.